1994

D1596178

A WOMAN'S MOURNING SONG

A WOMAN'S MOURNING SONG

bell hooks

HARLEM RIVER PRESS

NEW YORK   LONDON

Harlem River Press
P.O. Box 461, Village Station
New York, NY 10014

c/o Airlift Book Company
26 Eden Grove
London N7 8EF
England
Text copyright © 1993 bell hooks
Cover Design: Janice Walker

ISBN Cloth 0-86316-317-3
ISBN Trade 0-86316-318-1
1 2 3 4 5 6 7 8 9 0

Manufactured in the United States of America.

Contents

At Virginia Street Baptist church we sang sweet songs about dying. My favorite proclaimed: "One glad morning when this world is over, I'll fly away. I'll fly away. I'll fly away, oh glory, I'll fly away. When I die, hallelujah, bye and bye, I'll fly away." A joyous song, it brought a mood of rejoicing and celebration to death that has been a unique characteristic of traditional, Southern-rooted, diasporic African American ways of dying. I invoke the diaspora here because so many traditional ways of dying that were and are a part of black folks habits of being are informed by African, Caribbean, and South American approaches to dying, documented by cultural practices retained and cherished (found in places like those racially segregated black graveyards where one discovers beloved pictures, objects—glass jars, plates, even silverware—'cause anybody with good sense knows that death has to eat jus' like everybody else). Documenting this aspect of African American culture in *Flash of the Spirit: African and Afro-American Art and Philosophy*, art historian Robert Farris Thompson emphasizes the diasporic belief that graves should be covered with treasured objects used by the deceased, preferably those last touched or used: "In black North America the last-used objects of the dead are also believed to be specially charged with emanations, traces of the spirit. One can chart the continuity of this belief from plantation times (1845-65)—"Negro graves were always decorated with the last article used by the departed"—to St. Helena Island, Georgia, 1919, and Brownsville, Georgia, c. 1939 . . . " When African slaves took the Christian religion into their hearts and made Jesus and his father icons, giving them the human traits and qualities often bestowed on ancient familiar gods, death could no longer be just a moment for mourning and loss, it had to be also a time of celebration and rejoicing. One could not go to meet a friend with sorrow in the heart—since Jesus was a friend, one had to meet him with an open, loving, uplifted heart. Death meant union with the beloved. It had to be seen as a moment of pain and pleasure. The tears one shed had to be bitter and sweet.

It is this dynamic approach to dying, informed by notions of religious ecstasy, that black photographer James Van Der Zee documented in his many funeral portraits throughout this century. Carrying on the traditional colonial American desire for a 'mourning' picture—which was then a painting of the deceased—photography made it possible for everyone, irrespective of class, to possess images of the dead that could be placed on altars in homes, serving as constant reminders of that person's presence. Van Der Zee wanted his photographs of the dead to indicate that death was not a negative experience. In *The Picture Takin' Man* he recalled: "I made a great many funeral pictures. I always tried to insert something to break the gruesomeness of the picture and make it look more like the realities of life and the beauty of death. According to the scripture we should be more joyful at the going out and weep at the coming in." Continuing in the spirit of Van Der Zee in the catalogue for a recent show of her works "Then What? Photographs and Folklore," contemporary black woman photographer Carrie Mae Weems, in her own way, documents the reality of death as an experience that intensifies joy in the living, when she records this printed passage of Sister Kemp's prayer: "Oh heavenly Father, we thank you this day for allowing us yet another living day; you could have seen fit for to take us last night while we slept, but today—living—we saints gather, oh God, to glorify your name. Oh God, once I was out there in a world of sin, you sent Jesus for to be my friend, Oh Lawd, and J-e-s-u-s give me the courage to stare ole Satan down; yes he did!! Hallelu-jah!! Thank you Jesus, thank you Jesus, thank you Jesus. I know his power, saints, and I know his mercy— Amen, hum-de-la! I won't say church that I don't want to live. I'm a lie if I say I don't, but I'm telling you church, if the Lawd needs somebody, here am I, send me, I'll go. Amen! Amen! Amen! Raise your hands saints and say, Amen!" Many of the African peoples enslaved in North America brought with them traditions of Islamic mysticism, teachings which encouraged the seeker of truth to willingly give one's life to be joined with the Beloved. Such teachings were compatible with the Christian faith, which asserted that great love was shown by the willingness to give one's life.

The hard life of slavery also gave the enslaved African a different perspective on death. It could be viewed as solace for the suffering. In his poetic funeral sermon, "Go Down Death," James Weldon Johnson speaks of death as the comforter, the messenger of peace, who comes like "a falling star," a "welcomed friend" eager to bring rest to the worker who has "labored long" and who is tired and weary. Johnson admonishes: "Weep not, weep not, She is not dead; She's resting in the bosom of Jesus. Heart-broken husband— weep no more; Grief-stricken son—weep no more; Left-lonesome daughter—weep no more. She's only just gone home." Death, as spoken of in this sermon, is not an end but a transition that leads to a new beginning, to a different order of being. Intense mourning in traditional African American ways of dying, grief without ceasing, must be mediated by a sense of celebration. One rejoices to acknowledge the "rightness of dying ." One celebrates the passing of life not only to ease the transition of the dead but to make it known that the moment is also a time of reunion, when those who have been long separated come together. And for those who believe that the living leave us only to come back in a new way, there is even greater cause for celebration.

This unique relationship black people have to the dead and to the death experience has been shaped by the peculiar circumstances of life in white supremacist culture, particularly by the experience of living and dying in the historical period, euphemistically called "jim crow," of institutionalized racial apartheid in America. Many folks have forgotten what life was like for black people when racial apartheid meant that sick black folk could not easily gain access to medical care and were usually denied entrance into "white" hospitals. Folks have forgotten what it is like when a few white hospitals had their "black only" sections with not enough beds, and with little or no professional staff. And it takes "long memory" for folks to remember how precious black doctors and all black hospitals were to segregated black communities. Since the sick could not easily find care outside the home (such care often cost more than folks could afford), they were often cared for in homes. There, in domestic spaces among the living, those who did not make it passed away. Death, then, was no stranger. It was a familiar face, constantly present, staring life down.

Growing up in a small town in Kentucky where one of the first all-black hospitals was built and administered by black health care professionals (indeed Brooks Hospital carried the name of its founder, a caring black doctor many of us knew and loved). We knew, though, that there were only so many beds in that hospital, that they were most needed for folks who had a chance at getting well, and someone who was likely to die usually never entered, or was taken home. Hence, many of us grew up with the dying resting, waiting among us. There was easy death, and there was violent heart-rending death, and it took place right in front of the eyes of the living who could not forget death's power or ignore its fateful presence.

In our house we had a special room for the sick and dying; it was called the "middle room." Probably called this because it was a room close enough to the kitchen which was at the back of the house, yet near enough to the front of the house so that one could hear a cry of pain, a call of need. It was a place of transition, a room one could enter alive and leave dead. When I examine those experiences of childhood life, retrospectively, which had the greatest impact on my psyche, it was those moments wherein I watched the dying that made deep and profound imprints. I have always thought of death as "my witness" because it was in staring death down as a young girl that I learned to rebel without fear, knowing that if death could be faced then all dreaded experience could be confronted, lived through, overcome. I remember about death, then, that it was sometimes dreadful and at other times sweet (like Sister Ray passing during afternoon sleep, just like that, without sound or words, all quiet like). I wanted even then to stare death down, to gaze upon it unafraid, to know death intimately, love it even. When I left home, it was not long before I realized that country black folks had our own special way of dealing with dying, that those slaves and freed people who tenderly sang "come down, death, right easy" had laid the foundation for us to reflect on and know death in a unique way. One of the poems in this collection begins with the lines "death is always asleep in the middle room." It was like death had a location that frightened and fascinated.

Mine was a hurt and wounded childhood, at time the object of my father's uncontrollable rage, expressed in violent whippings, I learned to challenge him, to stand my ground and to survive because my first encounter with death showed it to be an experience that need not be feared or dreaded. Facing death, I was freed from the fear that fighting back could lead to destruction, to death. In her work on troubled and abused children psychoanalyst Alice Miller writes that individuals often survive extreme suffering in childhood because of the presence of "enlightened witnesses" who provide a "counterbalance for the cruelty they suffered." The cruelty I experienced did not crush my spirit because its most ominous threat was the possibility of losing one's life. To see death positively made resistance possible. And resistance ensured survival.

The first death I remember taking place in our house was that of my father's mother. Even though I was very young I vividly recall that day. Its strangeness was marked by mama's insistence that all of us (my sisters and brother) take a nap in the early afternoon—an uncommon event. Closed curtains, shut doors, darkened our bedroom, highlighting the presence of light through the doorway. In that room where Sister Ray, daddy's mother, had been lying sick for months, mystery was everywhere manifest. And I lay in my bed trying to listen for sounds that would explain the mystery. Hearing nothing, I dared to look. Mama was touching Sister Ray's face with her hands. Whether real or invented memory, I saw her tenderly close wide opened eyes, never saying a word. Still, I understood nothing. Not even when strange men entered the house with a stretcher talking and laughing. One of them caught me staring and leaned over my bed to tell me to stop pretending. He smelled of alcohol and sweet cologne. To this day, those smells call to mind death in the afternoon. Before these men arrived, everything had been serene and calm. Yet it was their presence that explained all that I had witnessed. I had looked at death and dying. Everything about that moment was full of tenderness and peace. Dead, Sister Ray no longer frightened me as she often had in her role as stern grandmother. After witnessing this event, which mama had believed her children were too young to see and understand, I wanted to ask a thousand questions about death and dying, but intuitively I knew it was important not to reveal all that I witnessed, to keep it as a private secret and use it to nurture my spirit.

Though there would be many deaths to face in the future, it was this experience that liberated me, that changed forever my relation to living. Witnessing what the old folks would call "a very easy death," I let go all fear of death and dying. This gentle passing became the standard by which I would measure all forms of dying. Whenever I was punished in ways that were meant to abuse and coerce, in the midst of whippings where crazed adults threatened to kill me, I was able to hold to principles and beliefs they did not share by reminding myself that death need not be feared or dreaded. I reminded myself that one need not compromise dedication to truth for fear of punishment, especially that which might appear life-threatening. This early imprint—the witnessing of an easy death—gave me courage. It was an inner secret that enabled me to bear pain and suffering yet hold on to the conviction that I could rebel and resist whenever necessary. No longer terrorized by fear of death and dying, I was able to live fully. Had this experience of death and dying happened in isolation, I might not have become a keen observer of African American ways of dying. It awakened in me an awareness of the significance of death and dying, impressing on my consciousness at an early age a positive feeling about death.

That positive feeling was reinforced by traditional Southern-rooted ways of thinking and being that enabled me and everyone else to look upon death as an important rite of passage that could be daily acknowledged, confronted, and talked about. As I grew older, I noticed how much grown folks, especially the elders, talked about death in daily conversations. Old black folks, who could not read or write, noted time and place of death by discussing events surrounding death and dying in great detail. It was a way to maintain history. Hearing narratives about the dead and dying in daily life conversation one could not forget that your time might be coming. Singing the song that lamented "soon, one morning death gonna creep into my room, oh my Lord, oh my Lordy, what shall I do," one knew that death was an event that had to be prepared for, that in knowing how to die one would also discover how to live.

Often when me and my siblings were bored and frustrated, mama would tell us again and again that "life is not promised." And with the constant repetition of this message she both reminded us of the reality of death and dying, while sharing that it was important to use this knowledge to find joy, pleasure, and fulfillment in the present. This profound insight had taken root in mama's psyche because of the many deaths she had witnessed. Losing her younger sister and a first child had taught her that death was no respecter of age, that at any moment life could be taken. Perhaps these experiences created in her that ambivalence which led her to try and protect her children when we were very young from the experience of death and yet to remind us of it constantly as we grew older.

It was a custom in our house and in the houses of family and friends to talk about the way one wanted to be treated when dead. Individuals planned their own funerals in great detail. Our mother was especially concerned with letting us know what should be done with her possessions if anything happened to her, telling us not only where to find things but also how to dress her. We were constantly aware that she might not always be with us. In this book of poems I dedicated "a sorrow song" to mama. I chose to write it in black vernacular to convey the playfulness and seriousness surrounding Southern black folks' approach to the subject of death and dying.

An atmosphere of celebration and mourning was always evoked in daily discussions of death and dying, but particularly when wakes and funerals were planned. Explaining the origin of the wake in the preface "Death through Some Other Windows" the editors of *Death: The Final Stage of Growth,* comment: "In the old days the dead could not be kept in the house. The body was thus left outside in the yard. In order to protect it from wild animals, the family stayed up with the dead . . ." Yet in diasporic black traditions one also stays with the dead to help guide their spirit to the other world, to keep them company, to have a last face-to-face conversation. Since in the old days black folks would travel long distances under difficult circumstances to pay their respects to the dead, the ancestors, and to the living who remain, there had to be much eating, drinking and overall revelry to fully, ritually respond to death. Burying the dead was only one aspect of the ceremonial rites of passage enacted during such times. Death often enabled reunion and reconciliation. A time of forgiveness, it often became that event which enabled confession, a sharing of all the issues that might, in another cultural experience, take place in therapy. For this reason black folks saw times of dying as healing moments, as well as times of mourning.

In traditional Southern-rooted black life, funerals have been, and are, times where the living show their regard by how they take care of the dead, how they "lay them out ." Hence details of dress are important as is the quality of casket, etc. It is equally important what one wears to a funeral. Ultimately it is the ceremony, indicating whether the deceased is loved and respected, that determines how they will be remembered. When Baba, my mother's mother, died shortly before her ninetieth birthday, her funeral did not take place in a church (after much family discussion) because she had rebelled against churchgoing as a young woman after witnessing hypocrisy at services (folk's backbiting and talking ugly). Her coffin was surrounded by tulips, one of her favorite flowers. They reminded us of the beauty of her gardens. That day I thought about Alice Walker's essay "In Search of Our Mother's Gardens," for she speaks about the importance of this display of black female artistry. Remembering her mother in ways that I remember Baba, Walker nostalgically recalled: "Whatever she planted grew as if by magic, and her fame as a grower of flowers spread over three counties. Because of her creativity with her flowers, even my memories of poverty are seen through a screen of blooms—sunflowers, petunias, roses, dahlias, forsythia, spirea, delphiniums, verbena . . . and on and on." Whenever I see flower gardens, I remember my grandmother. To me her spirit is everywhere. Often I say to Mama, "Baba's spirit is everywhere. I feel her presence among the tulips and it brings me joy." Her funeral was joyous. The moment I remember most of this sweet ceremony was when the preacher told us not to grieve about her passing but to rejoice for it was no longer a pleasure for her to remain alive in a world where "her choicest friends were gone." His words made sense not just in reference to Baba's life but as a reminder to us, the living, that the deepest joy in life is found in communion with those whom we love. It is important to be able to recognize one's "choicest" friends, to be able to call their names. And so we mourned—and yet our grief was also a celebration.

In his essay "Dying as the Last Stage of Growth" (published in the anthology *Death: The Final Stage of Growth*) Mwalimu Imara speaks eloquently of the way we can use knowledge of dying as a way to guide how we live. He declares: "Living to the fullest, to capacity, to transcendence, demands that we live lives of awareness, mutual self-communication and direction ." Traditional African Americans ways of thinking and talking about death and dying helped create a lived experience where we could accept the reality of death and live life accordingly. So often the precariousness of life for black folks in a white supremacist, capitalist patriarchy reminds us constantly of the importance of the moment, of living in the here and now. When this knowledge is linked with that understanding of self that enables us to know who we are and how we want to live in the world, situations of oppression and exploitation can be resisted and we can actively transform our world.

In the black church tradition it is important that the believer be able to stand before a community of faith and testify so that all who hear can be affirmed and guided. Closing this piece, I find myself most inarticulate when I try to share how I have been able, throughout this life I am living to use the knowledge that "life is not promised," to be courageous, to take risks. Indeed, as an insurgent black intellectual, cultural critic, feminist theorist, poet and visual artist, I feel that I would be fundamentally unable to occupy subject positions that require me to assert transgressive critical thoughts that may or may not be popular without debilitating fear if I had not learned early on to cherish each moment of my life, and see it as crucial that I express my gratitude by living fully. For me, that means with commitment and devotion to trust. With death as my guide I can take risks, for I am not afraid of dying to old habits, old beliefs. Imara reminds us: "When we abandon the old familiar patterns of life, whether voluntarily or involuntarily, we always have a sense of risk-taking. When the new situation involves changes which may have grave consequences for our future well-being, the level of anxiety is bound to be great. Abandoning old ways and breaking old patterns is like dying, at least dying to old ways of life for an unknown new life of meaning and relationships. But living without change is not living at all, not growing at all. Dying is a precondition for living." Just as mama's words of "life is not promised" were meant to remind us to choose wisely in our actions and to nurture a joyous spirit, Imara shows how our capacity to respond creatively and constructively to life changes is to a grave extent shaped by our ability to face the reality that we are at each moment of our life in stages of transition that are, inevitably, preparations for dying.

I am writing this essay at a moment in my life when I am undergoing a crisis, considering major life changes. A year ago, a number of people in my life died unexpectedly, from unpredictable causes. They were young. Their deaths gave me "pause." These confrontations with death and dying were bold reminders, compelling me to look at the direction of my life and honestly acknowledge spaces of lack and longing, spaces of unfulfillment. In response to the many questions I asked myself then, I am changing the direction of my life. Many times in the past months I have wished that just the sheer strength of knowing that "life is not promised"—that death is always happening—would make it clear how I/we must act and what I/we must do. Indeed, such knowledge may simply motivate and intensify our search for understanding, for right livelihood, yet we must still struggle for answers, face the unknown, grope towards the new future without any clear guidance or plan. This is difficult. Only last night, I told mama that I felt as though I was a spinning top, that I felt afraid. I reminded her of how often she used to say to us as children "life is not promised," telling her how when I need that special push to move forward, I nurture myself with these words.

When we spoke last night, she told me that one of my childhood friends was home because her mother had died. I remembered with her, how as a child I often disturbed her patience by saying: "I want to die before you because I can't imagine life without you." I ask her, "Mama, do you remember how you would say 'little girl, I'll be long gone and you will live' " and I say, "See, Mama, life is showing us that might be so." Together, we lament how hard it is to accept the mystery of dying, why some are called when we think it's not their time. "Well ," I tell her, "it's another way to think about what we mean when we say life is not promised, that you cannot be thinking that just 'cause you young there is no death." We laugh and talk about how we both want to be ready when the time comes, how we both want to feel that we have truly lived.

the woman's mourning song

i cry
i cry high
this mourning song
my heart rises
sun in hand
to make the bread
i rise
my heavy work hand
needs
the voice of many singers
alone
the warmth of many ovens comfort
the warrior in me returns
to slay sorrow
to make the bread
to sing the mourning song
i cry high
i cry high
i cry
the mourning song
go away death
go from love's house
go make your empty bed

the guard of captive hearts

bitter sleep
in which nightmares roam
wild horses ride me down
one after the other
they bid me confess or die
i am as she
the chosen one
ridden weary
ridden until she drops
her loa a bringer of darkness
the love of women
is the beginning of wisdom
they cry
and in so saying
are silenced
to speak no more
driven by ghede's chariot underground
ghede whose body is covered in ash
ghede the womanizer
the sustained one
the eater of human flesh
mounted by he
she is transformed
chagall's blue horse
the unimagined one

a sorrow shaded between black and white
in her madonna arms
lies the remembrance of innocence

the body inside the soul

i am listening for your footsteps death
i am waiting here
with my young hammer
here with my little knife
i shall pound your fingers
as you open the door
i shall grind them like corn
i shall make bread
i shall sing a praise song
a song my mother taught me
the earth it is round
there is no edge
there is no way to fall off

the heart obsidian

against earth core
the stone that is all our being
lies buried
shrouded in the burnt ashes
of our heart cloth
damp rooted in a living culture
my father's eyes
are gray with time
we build the funeral pyre
we light the first spark
gone now the land
gone now the memories
gone now the healing touch
we are alone now
we are alone now
alone now
our sorrow soaring
lone bird in solitary flight

alcheringa

dream time
time without time
never never land
in the face of our mother
a great black bear
closing in winter
the crops under the snow weep
i go about the house
sad all the time
for at the grave of our dead brother
whose face we never saw
a voice spoke to us
embraced us with the knowledge
of who we were
before we became ourselves in this life
we heard of an endless land
world without boundaries
a space open enough for peace
we returned to our habits lonely
unsure of how to go about
the daily meditations

famine of memory

the dead we dig up
to find ourselves
carved faces
handkerchiefs of grief
bathed in sweat
as we climb each secret ladder
ongoing loss
this origin search
names without memory
another headless body
dreaming its end
beginning rung
our sorrow tastes of death
a grasping heavy hunger
falls upon us

at the mouth of the cave

sleeping
and the heart growing still
the throat gasping for air
all this dreamless slumber
hastens death
beside a lover of long years
i lie cold and stiff
hard body of desire
awakening flesh
to enter each crevice
bliss and the moist tongue
wet the water of thirst
in the silent cave
life resurrected
the third day
the coming messenger

poem from the first life

in the first life
i was uncertain
i was a snake with eyes closed
with no hands
i was only one body
slow moving in the dark

alone in my heart
digging a house of dirt and stone
a temple to all unknowing
there to worship
there to sing
there to pray
there to wait the end
all things fall into

revelation

i wake in the cave
out of cold sleep
into the illumined night
dark clarity of suns
shining i within i
faceless face of the watcher
guiding zar
angel of beginning and end
we dream this apocalypse
elijah satan and the burning heat
standing enflamed love
heart in hand

hymn to the beloved

away from the one
a sorrow pierced my heart
i sang always
one song of longing
to return again
to enter once more the divine circle
to dance in the ring of love
to be joined in an endless harmony
bound by heart strings drawn tight

towards the one i journey
led by a music of souls
hearing only one heart crying
one harp playing in the night
by moving hands unseen

for found fathers

i have seen an old man facing death
numbering his days
as the weaver her threads
he leaves behind no memories
not even a name
by which the living can call his spirit back
he will inhabit no more bodies
he dreams narcissus
the clear water
the face no longer seen
lost in an endless present
he stirs the last cup
wanders slowly home
through dark familiar rain
to a cold hand
an open door
and a stairway he can no longer climb

unnamed our search

i come slowly
through the doors of locked rooms
behind them worlds i have made
hands bare crude tools
no sound at all
but the steadying
beat of a heart
cold hammer pounding
the proper way to nail
one sharp quick stroke
our father's hand
guiding us
away from love's touch
into a new world
we must discover again and again
the way home

not to be a woman who waits

she declares
that she will not be a woman who waits
watching for signs of lovers
coming and going
no anchor safe harbor refuge
to be returned to
no she has other obsessions

in her nightmares
she is wounded
it is a family crime
loved ones stare silent unforgiving
ignore her pleas for mercy
she is locked in a room
they tell her to be patient
to take heart
to cherish all moments of surrender

an account of the fall

in this silence
that is not unlike death
he comes
with the word
wrapped in cloth-dyed cotton
colored with the earth
spun by the unseen hands of women
whose veiled faces are a hidden speech
he will never know
and so he professes to love
who practices deceit
in this way evil came into the world

holy this communion

in that sacred space
no woman can enter
the angel messenger comes
bringing good news
take eat
the bread
in memory of his body
take drink
the wine
to recapture the living blood
in reverence
we tarry together
worshipping
the slain hunter
the lost cannibal

turning your face away

sweet daughters of jerusalem
remember your sisters
dark and comely
braiding their hair
into thick tapestries
mapping world history
in each movement
traces of the love
you did not share
threaded red and weary
piercing memory
wets our flesh
with abandonment
the shaved heads of bondage
the shared secret of captivity
and the death they take us to
public and unmourned betrayal

against the darkness

in this house of stone
we do not sing
we sleep
our bodies trapped
in a death that is not our making
we remember life
the sound of children playing
their voices sharp
and crazy with happiness
smell of flowers
in the night air
and in our minds wanderings
what name for such fragrance
only that it fills the nostrils
with a sense of peace and contentment
we will never know again
we remember a love song
words and music
not a voice of longing and passion
but of high unreachable bitter grief
we remember it now
slow choked voice of the singer
reaching through our memories
like an out stretched hand
and we are close together again

our bodies
a living rock
poised against the darkness

coming fall

in the catch of seasons
dead septembers lie scattered
flat feet of dry leaves
wet winds press
against the heart
peel back desire
dust of burnt leaves
love's heavy odor
mounts the air
erotic sweeps
the coming winter

portions of a negative

pinched white edges
man rays eyes
sunlit
pierce through objects
cut in half dreams
dangles from his wrist
a heart piece
worn like a watch
telling time
one hour
after hours
a darkness enters
in this woman's body
human light transforms the images
merges
one photographs
a studio
breasts
canvasses
the hidden cunt
behind gustav klimt's
world torn bodies
of raped women
disembodied limbs
hung in tragic poses

in whose blood waters
portraits surface
colors brilliant
opaque
translucent
souls glitter
as they lament
love's eager descent

the lotus hook

the mother who loved her daughter
but could not love her feet
sleeps without sleeping
eater of dream fruit
she lies content
her body a many petalled lilly
hiding pain in ecstasy
she pulls the cloth tighter
binding grief
stitches in pure silk
the little shoes
silences the dancers heart

they wake in my sleep

the dead know one another
they say
wearing one face in meeting
speaking through one mouth
kneeling in the dirt
sun on their face and back
searching heat and dirt
for the bodies of our dead
longing to reveal the mystery
three million years old
the bones of young ethiopia
running beautiful and free
yet if these bones rise
who will carry them back to god
place them in the nigger cemetery
where black don't lay with white
yet if these bones rise
what spirit will come
to free them
locked behind the clear glass
and printed words
slaves once more to history

r i f f s

riffs
a recurring lyric
hillbilly sound of crackers
whose poverty
carries the voice of hate
country western music
all day long
the radio voice
grand ole opry
and the hanging song
dances of white flesh
against white flesh
saturday night
sound of soul
short sweet hours
we bring you music
a white man
with a black voice
announcing your tune
the nashville sound of randy
all night long
riffs
a memorial to louie armstrong dying
his trumpet sound
our well of memory

leadbelly
bleeding his guts in song
taste of moonshine
colors all our grief
and love that music
makes the night sweet

we remember hiroshima

(for the hibakusha)

I
smells of burning
carry the weeping sound
the wailing song
tortured as we ran
as we flung our bodies
in the dirt
as we tried to hide
as we ran
captured and the invisible fire
still wakes us in the night
tearing our flesh
as we remember hiroshima
and the ones who lived
to die again
and again
and again

we remember hiroshima

II
in our silence is a returning fire
always we entered this memory alone
telling our grief to no one

covering our scars with shame
hiding the map of terror
the wounds that do not heal
the wounds that cannot be seen
again another august
another invisible fire
burning in our sleep
above the flames
we speak our cry to the world

they warmakers

words will not stop war
will not stop pain falling
like the sound of your voice
to one who is deaf
and looking another way
lips cannot be read in darkness
in the black sky of nagasaki
death's ray is white and burning
the world where atoms are made
is sacred to those
who no longer guard what they have conquered
who lay their nightmares to rest in clear day
among fields of growing rice
in the hearts of newborns
they waste love
they take and take life
they carry the world into sleep

in that place somewhere there is revolution

they say
men die there
and blood is all around
even in drinking cups
that graffiti is written on tents
and in the earth with dark red ink
they say
children are born there
growing like roses
on the vines and branches of dead bodies

and we say
our souls bear witness
to death that ends
to a morning that comes
to new light

seeing you then
angolan freedom fighter

on the battlefield
gun in hand
child in belly
i have never killed a man
on the battlefield
we hoe and plow
gun in hand
i have never killed a man
baby on lap
stern face mama
gun in hand
i will kill and go blind
i will kill and never
see a falling body
i will kill
and there will be no one
to cover the eyes of my child

vietnam ending
as they bury their dead

to dig
the grave of a people
it is the way death is
knowing no names
this hole in the earth
where we come together as one

it rains
and so the tears of women
cease their falling
no longer do we dream
of a new land
but wait the day
when our bones too
shall cry out
against the striking of the blade
as they lay dead after dead upon us

leaving lebanon

fleeing
we have no time
to bury our dead
we leave
broken limbed crushed bones
shocked eyes opened wide
we leave them
without peace
without memory of grieving loved ones
hovering near the still sleep
from which they will not return
without kisses or farewells
we leave them
because we must
fleeing
we have no time
to bury our dead
we weep as we run
we run weeping
we flee death
searching for a mourning time

no more firewater

we do not leave the land
the land leaves us
we watch
as they who know not
the soothing weight of the earth
upon the body
as hands which have not yet
found a way to speak
take the land
our men they do not weep
nor do our women cry
it is because we believe
the land will someday return
in the earth we are waiting
when the rains come
we will rise

the bloody ground

we trod
the bloody ground
our feet
search the path
for a new land
the bodies of our dead
await this coming
dressed in the ritual costumes
of the motherland
we go to greet them
recalling their native tongue
the rhythm beat into the drum
beat into our soul
so the drum in us moves
a throbbing heartbeat
inside a weary people
seeking home

indian summer blues

again that same longing
no more complete and absolute
open space
in a land without indians
whose wells are dry
whose prairies no one remembers
whitman sang america
i seem to hear his solemn voice
shake my sleep
as i dream each day
the possibility of unknown horror
each dream the same memory of grief
echoes that bring back
cheers of a people
whose soldiers come home from war
the wail of slave mothers
whose children go sold
to the highest bidder
and somewhere among magnolias
women who dance
clothed in romance dream
sure of love's constancy
when death blossoms
sweet flowering time
fragrance of the first remembered kiss

save now we pray

i want to go down
once more to the river
hear them black angels
sing hosanna
see those bodies go down
hear them hallelujah cries
amen and thank you jesus
i want to go down
into the dark and muddy water
hear them voices
moaning low praying sounds
to suffer surrender be free
to suffer surrender be free
to suffer surrender be free
to suffer surrender be free
i want to go down

dreaming the unborn

i know how you
will feel inside me
child of the unborn
the pain that will come
like the knife wound
i have watched you
standing in the shadows
singing
i wait in silence
bleeding your coming

abandonment

her man done gone
left her
she just be
sitting on the porch rocking
she got nothing to say
to nobody
some folks say
she never moves
from that chair
that she always
be waiting
other folks say
her mind been
slipping ever since
the day he left
me i say
she be just like
a dead person
someone should walk
upon that porch
and shut them eyes

over home

pictures of all of us
in antique frames
round rectangular square
margaret in blue
whose favorite color
against the brownness of her skin
a dress of dreams
we all wore feathers in our hats then
birds of beauty
we smiled at the camera eye
and these here
on this wall
are my sons
dressed in the uniforms of war
smiling seductive grins
all that death hidden from them then
they wrote to me of home
like rachel i wept
for lost children
i would not see against
papa was so fair she said
the daguerreotype
fragile with age
i have no words to tell you grief
just look at him

papa so fair
and in this corner
unknown women
wearing dark red lipstick
lust scented perfumes
skirts hiding their bony knees
sailors and grinning faces in nightclubs
the family extended into slavery
freedom and the camera eye
taking in all time
turning the past back
so we glimpse our stolen souls
eyes bright with unshed tears

the interior wall

friends left behind
ghosts of bad dreams
that stalk our paths
breath of dead lovers
who wake us with a hot heat
and what he wanted
was no more than to talk
and then to continue the talk
an old exchange
of kindness for kindness
big mama's shoes
side by side under the bed
grief like swollen feet
stands in them
if i touch you now
what will i look forward to
in future years of longing
mama was not a virgin bride
but she wanted to be
wanted to walk that aisle
unencumbered by memories
of the first man the second
the dream of only having known
one man in a world of manyness
his body an old coat

a worn nightgown cherished
but somehow gone the original beauty
his chair grandfather remains
silent and stuffed with memories
hand that held us lingers there
invisible in time
i sit trying to fill the space of years
facing the aged wallpaper paint
that once green now nameless peels
cracks open fantasy
to let in light
from the interior wall

forgotten time

inside death's door
there lies waiting
an awakened sleeper
one who walks these floors
each night
searching for keys
hidden money
a worn prayer book
in her old age
she finds time
to remember god
talks to him
about her lost pride
and dignity
mumbling that life
it shouldn't be like this
to see one's mind
slipping into youth
and out again
the first marriage
the second baby
many deaths
glimpses of early black life
down home in georgia
swamps and cottonfields

riding in a wagon
driven by a white mule
come west
following the people
in the big house
collards planted
in the front yard
her legs growing thick
like tree trunks
hardly walking
silent and ashamed
she crawls into memory

to honor the big mamas

the women who walk behind
swing children on their hips
bring water
carry filled baskets
placed elegantly on their heads
they are not practicing ladies
their bodies are tired and weary
from long unending labor
their steps are straight
for no one waits to catch them
should they stumble
no hands reach out
to break their fall
they stand alone
with death and sorrow
they have measured pain
in their cups
they hold their courage in
rub hard their hands in soapy wash
clean and sweep with weary arms
bake warm corn cakes
and honey bread
they are not ashamed
all the joy in their laughter
carries the sound of a proud heart

walking into exile

heavy in her black coat
scarf pulled tight
round her face
face that is blank
face without memories
holding together
the self she is sure to lose
her fingers clinging tight
a child's terror
a child's fear
that all separation is death
this still life body pleads
holds a silent wake
mourning love's absence
the loss of intimacy
hands that touched
without fear or shame
eyes that parting wept
now she is no where
in her mind
all time has ended
she has arrived at a place
where all she is
all she belongs to
all that remains is hidden

closed behind a wall
her new image
a blank face
a face without memories

another mourning

i came to see if death would change you
if instead of your bright eyes
i would find buttons from an old shirt handpainted
or better yet diamonds
bright and glittering in the funeral chapel
or maybe i would find the sockets empty
like a clock with no face
and only a memory of time
the living have made of you
someone i did not know
a stranger passing through
noticed but unknown
a sleepwalker afraid of the dark
with eyes closed
not knowing that you will never awake
that you will never again
stare deep into the face of love
or weep at our departing
not knowing you go alone
that you will not find me there waiting

deep ongoing this loss

my soul mourns
the death of love
i wait outside prison gates
in the long day
my hands pressed against the sadness
against the pain
these dark walls that keep me from you
too cold to weep
too weary to remember
by heart i have learned grief
over and over again
this trapped wounded naked hurt
that has become our body

a sorrow song

(for mama)

when i die
leave this old fur coat to lula jones
everytime i wore it
she grinned at me
as if to say
this time
this time i will take
what should rightfully be mine
when i die
i want my oldest girl
to have all the jewelry
i was her first queen
adored above all others
when i die
there will be no money
for yall to fuss over
i have spent it all
when i die
split the dishes among you
if no one wants them
give them to the church
take the old clothes
give them to the rag lady
or burn them whatever

i shall not miss a thing
when i die
dress me up fine
i have hung my good black dress
in the right hand corner of the closet
in my top dresser drawer
i have left a clean slip
a new pair of silk stockings
a small purse
one tube of lipstick
and my favorite perfume
when i die
i want no one to grieve
for it will be
my eyes closed to familiar faces
my arms left lonely
my voice that will no longer
long to sing
when i die
i want no one to grieve
for the sorrow will all be mine

mourning pictures

down
down
this path of sorrow
i walk
birds and their songs
flee from me
beat their anguished wings
go way go way
the sound against my heart
this too lonely feeling
sighs the sleeping body
death and life one way
the grave
our final nest of love

companions of the cave

I
forever
awakened
one comes
to join the secret order
drenched with longing
to lie down
in the bed
of no return

II
the abyss of surrender
how she takes my hand
how she holds me
how she tenderly caresses
that place in my heart
where the assassin
longs to enter

when the sharp edge of love
pierces my soul
i do not mourn
this passing of one into another
i give my life over to death willingly
a sign the devoted one
without limits or boundaries

III
wearing the assassin's mask
they stand
before the door
of a closed heart
breaking the wanderer's path
their sorrow a true wilderness
untamed and unconquered love
aflame with victory
they pierce the air with fire

IV
heavy laden wearer of wool
each wanderer moves in desert heat
in search of the secret order
dancing ones who leave behind
bodies spent with love
as they flee life
falling weary
at the feet of the assassin

V
inside
desert wilderness
the cry of love
is heard
circles the air
from afar
sounds over the mountain
call the one who journeys home

VI

where is the beloved one

who is all heart

giver of rain

dream maker

where do you hide

our love grows cold

we faint from thirst

we can no longer remember

is there no end to desire

VII
in the darkness of one heart
we await the sound
that is both end and beginning

at each moment of surrender
the secret for which
we have searched
is found

VIII

come

from your hiding place

your desert heat

i wait for you

come

with your burning body

your bright eye

come

into the cave of treasures

come

forsaken heart

without you

each cold night

tears open sleep

IX
at the top of this pyramid
stands the messenger
one more wounded one
trapped by the assassin
and a love that shows no mercy

in a world with no mercy
the dancing ones
cut off their feet
turn legs into sticks
give each crippled body a cane

in a world with no dance
no heart is moved to longing
no wet love comes to wash the holy feet
to make the dead rise from ash into song

from under sacred earth
spirits rise
birds of paradise
bursting with renewed song
call the dancers from their midnight sleep
loosen the captive heart

X
beloved
i call you

heart that burns

beloved
i call you

soul that bears witness

beloved i call you to come

XI

inside each wounded place
black serpents rest
sorcerers of dreams
before the shrine of memory
that love that was my flesh burns
ash covered i sit
an early morning wake
longing for your return

XII
caught out
the arms of the assassin
reach each corner of the heart
i dream night everywhere
another dark face against yours
within words i trace the silence
moving into your body
holding on in this reality
before light breaks
and all is forgotten time

XIII
as surely as fragile
the shattering glass
so the dreamed about heart breaks
scattering unrecovered pieces
each bit bleeding into memory
the salt taste sweat of your flesh
as her tongue takes each dark opening
finding there love's lingering trace

XIV

we enter the cave one body
sure that the dark
is a spirit dwelling place
sure that the assassin
will enter here
call our names
take each private part
and make our being whole

houses of mourning

in this house
are silent watchers
awaiting resurrection
the soul in flight
the soul fleeing
this lost haven
that is our body

in this house
are women wailing
crying high
the mourning song
chanting glory
on the other side
chanting victorious
surrender

the last song

(for the paiutes who gave us another way)

within my hands
i hold the magic seed
let us eat and drink together
our time will not be long

within my voice
i carry the magic sound
our song of sorrow
our dance of praise

within my heart
i house the hidden flower
fragrance of morning
dew of nightfall

that we may sleep sound
remembering always
this time together

Other Books

by bell hooks

Black Looks

Race and Representation

by bell hooks

In these twelve new essays, hooks digs ever deeper into the personal and political consequences of contemporary representations of race and ethnicity within a white supremicist culture. Whether discussing reconstructing Black masculinity, academic debates over "difference," the portrayal of Black women in popular film, or the relationship between African Americans and Native Americans, hooks consistently demonstrates the incisive intelligence and passion for justice that prompted *Publishers Weekly* to dub her one "of the foremost black intellectuals in America today."

Breaking Bread

Insurgent Black Intellectual Life

by bell hooks
with Cornell West

"A series of dialogues between and interviews with two of the foremost black intellectuals in America today, this volume is of enormous importance and offers rewarding reading . . . West and hooks talk frankly about the difficult necessity of moving beyond the academy to reach an audience in the black community at large. Much of their talk focuses on the violence done to the black community by consumer capitalism, by rampant market forces that have eroded the traditional institutions of support within the community, replacing them with a Big Mac and designer sneakers. Both are suspicious of the easy appeal of certain brands of black nationalism currently fashionable, but their analysis of those trends is balanced and convincingly argued."
— *Publishers Weekly*

Yearning

Race, Gender, and Cultural Politics

by bell hooks

Crossing disciplinary boundaries in major debates on post-modern theory, cultural criticism, and the politics of race and gender, hooks warns that fashionable infatuation with "discourse" about "difference" is dangerously detachable from struggles against racism, sexism and cultural imperialism.

Winner of the 1991 Before Columbus Foundation's American Book Award.

"hooks applies her 'critical yet supportive' model to a myriad of relationships and situations, many of which engage some of today's most dynamic issues."
— *Ms. Magazine*

Feminist Theory

From Margin to Center

by bell hooks

In this modern classic, bell hooks suggests that feminists must account for the full diversity of female experience, including black women's role in shaping feminist theory. A sweeping examination of the core issues of sexual politics: sisterhood; men; power; work; education; violence; parenting; sexist oppression; and feminist revolution. hooks' work challenges the women's movement and pushes it forward.

"An important work, essential for women's and black studies collections."
— *Library Journal*

Talking Back
Thinking Feminist, Thinking Black

by bell hooks

A strong and uncompromising investigation of feminist consciousness in daily life, political organizing, intimate relationships, education, and white supremacy within the women's movement, exposing the points where the public and private meet.

"Largely because of hooks' style—more like conversation around the kitchen table on a summer evening than academic prose—highly controversial and radical thoughts seem obvious. Working for change becomes not only challenging and exciting, but also productive."
— *DARE*

Ain't I A Woman

Black Women and Feminism

by bell hooks

A groundbreaking work of feminist theory which examines sexism in the black community and racism in the women's movement, and shows that progressive struggles have significance only when they recognize the complex relations between different forms of oppression.

"This exciting book reveals bell hooks to be a lucid, persuasive writer and an extraordinarily penetrating and original thinker . . . Her book should be widely read, thoughtfully considered, discussed, and finally acclaimed for the real enlightenment it offers for social change."
— *Library Journal*

"One of the twenty most influential women's books written in the last twenty years!"
— *Publishers Weekly*

bell hooks (Gloria Watkins) grew up in Kentucky. She received her B.A. at Stanford University and her Ph.D. at the University of California, Santa Cruz.

Currently, she is a professor at Oberlin College in the Departments of English and Women's Studies; previous-ly, she spent three years as as associate professor in the African American Studies Department at Yale University.

bell hooks received the Before Columbus Foundation's 1991 American Book Award for Yearning: Race, Gender, and Cultural Politics. *In 1990, The American Studies Association Critic's Choice Panel chose* Talking Back *as one of the most outstanding recent books in the area of Educational Studies.*